MW00585421

HAUNTED KEY WEST

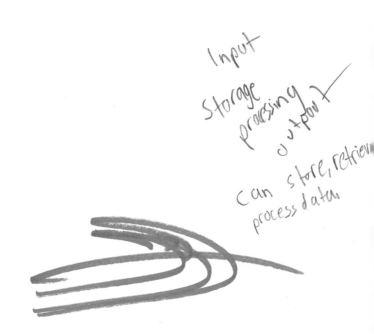

Input
Storage
processing
output

Can store, retrieve
process data

DAVID L. SLOAN

PHANTOM PRESS
KEY WEST

Editing services: dorothydrennen.com

Inquiries: david@phantompress.com

ISBN: 978-0-9789921-5-6

LOCAL LEGEND

PHOTO: ROB O'NEAL

An estimated 100,000 people are buried in the Key West Cemetery. The cemetery was created in 1847 after a storm washed the bodies from an earlier burial ground near the Southernmost Point. The dead currently outnumber the living by a ratio of 4:1.

CONTENT

Content

AUTHOR'S NOTE

Thanks for picking up this copy of Haunted Key West. The title was originally released in 2003 and was discontinued in 2010. It came back from the dead in 2015 - new and improved.

This edition features the same stories as the original book. The content has been enhanced with more than 50 new photos, a dozen one-pagers dedicated to local legends, updates on haunted locations that have moved or changed hands, and a fresh cover.

I have also included a bonus story about Count Von Cosel and some rarely seen photos, as well as suggestions on other books to check out if you enjoy the haunted history of our island. But for now, enjoy Haunted Key West.

Happy Hauntings.

David L. Sloan

PREFACE

When I first became involved in the ghost business, I never imagined that it would lead to a book, much less a sequel. Years later I find myself with more hauntings than pages in the book, as I decide which ghosts are crying out most loudly for their stories to be told.

The answer to the question "Do ghosts really exist?" is not important. Some people will believe and others will not. It has never been my intention to change people's beliefs — I prefer to leave personal beliefs to the individual and the ghost. Ghosts have taken the country by storm over the past decades; multiple ghost tours have popped up in many major cities, and ghosts continue to be featured in movies, print media, and television. The ghosts' stories are waiting to be told, and more stories are unfolding as we collectively become more receptive.

A favorite question of mine when interviewing potential ghost hunt guides is: "Do you believe in ghosts?" Some candidates do, some do not, and most fall somewhere in between. After a month or two of touring, they are all believers.

Brant Voss joined my old company as a tour guide early in 2003. June was a busy month, and Brant was conducting five or six ghost tours each week. On the Fourth of July, Brant became a true believer. Brant had enjoyed the afternoon snorkeling with his girlfriend, Karen. When they returned home to get ready for the fireworks and a night on the town, he was unable to find his red, white and blue bandanna and matching shorts. They tore apart the closet and looked in every drawer and cabinet, but the items were nowhere to be found. Brant gave up and wore something else. When they returned home later that night, the red, white and blue bandanna lay neatly folded on top of the matching shorts in the center of their bed. That same night Karen heard a voice calling her name; Brant was asleep, but their dogs Ralph and Alice barked hysterically at the mirror.

All of the guides have had similar experiences, and they have come to realize that the ghosts are communicating with them and through them to make their stories known.

The stories in this book are based on firsthand accounts I have collected over the years; I have included additional information from the sources listed within the book. Most names have been changed as a courtesy.

Whether you are a believer, a skeptic, or something in between, I hope that you will enjoy reading these stories as much as I enjoyed collecting them. They probably won't scare you to death or send shivers down your spine like the big Hollywood movies - but if you think about the stories as you close your eyes at night, you just might encounter lost spirits trying to make their stories known. After all, this is Key West, and stranger things have happened.

State of Florida Archives

THE
WATER WITCH
OF
APPELROUTH LANE

State Of Florida Archives

The presence of fresh water wells made Key West a strategic location for Native Americans, pirates, and early settlers. Neighborhoods were formed based on their proximity to a fresh water source, but the life-giving water could be a source of sorrow when the wells spread disease and caused death. Most of the island's old wells have been capped, but some long-departed residents still search for their locations. The Water Witch of Appelrouth Lane is one of those spirits.

Appelrouth Lane is known for upscale bars, restaurants, and lounges serving up refreshments, but stories continue to emerge about a different kind of spirit who is looking for more than a drink. They call her The Water Witch of Appelrouth Lane.

Joe McGuire emerged from the nightclub and lit a smoke. Appelrouth Lane is only one block long, running between Duval and Whitehead in one of the busiest parts of town. It had been another busy night at the club, Wax, and the mostly vacant lane provided a sharp contrast to the thumping beats of DJ Peter Worth and the throngs of people dancing to the rhythm inside. Joe grabbed his scooter from the thirty or so parked outside, turned the key, hit the ignition, eased off the kickstand, and slowly cruised toward Whitehead Street. He hoped that he might have more luck with the ladies at the Parrot than he had been having in any other bar that night. Little did he know that the next lady he would encounter was a bit of a legend on Appelrouth.

A plainly dressed woman flagged him down from the wall behind the San Carlos Institute. It appeared that she had been crying. Joe slowed his scooter to see if everything was OK. "Do you need a ride somewhere?" he asked. The girl didn't answer, but disappeared right before his eyes.

Nobody is quite sure about the identity of this mysterious lady. Unlike most ghosts, she does not stick to one place, preferring instead to visit locations up and down the lane. Her presence first became known at the Twisted Noodle, the restaurant formerly known as the 416, and currently a local favorite called 2 Cents.

Monroe County Public Library

416 Appelrouth Lane in the 1900s. 2 Cents restaurant now occupies the structure where guests and staff report regular encounters with the mysterious water witch.

"We started out serving dinner only, so it was late in the afternoon before I came in to set everything up," explained Michael, a former employee of the Noodle. "The first time it happened, I was stocking the coolers behind the bar when I noticed a young lady walking toward the back of the restaurant's patio. Normally I would have yelled that we were not opening for another hour. She looked kind of cute, so I told her if she wanted she could have a drink at the bar. She didn't respond. I noticed that she was wearing a long dress and that she had a bucket in her hand. I thought it was a purse at first, but as I watched, she headed back to the planter by the big banyan tree and acted like she was getting water from a well. When she passed back in my direction, I asked if I could help her with anything, but again she acted oblivious to me and just walked toward the front gate. I followed a minute later to see what was up, but when I reached the front gate it was still locked."

Michael and the other employees encountered the ghost on several other occasions. Every account depicted a pretty young woman in a long dress walking to a well that was not there and fetching water in her bucket before disappearing, while refusing to acknowledge anyone the entire time.

"We named her Noel, like a play on words for 'no well.' The most peculiar thing about her is that she doesn't look like a ghost," Michael explained. "She appears like anybody else who would walk into the restaurant, with the exception of the bucket – and her ability to vanish. Some of my friends are convinced she is a witch. Here is the strangest part - when we were remodeling a few months ago at the Noodle, we tore out the planters and found the base of a well right where she was fetching the water. That's how she became known as the water witch."

Though the Twisted Noodle is gone, Noel has remained. In addition to 2 Cents, her ghost visits the lane's guesthouse, Virgilio's Lounge and the club formerly know as Wax. Tim Schwarz, who worked at the 420 bar, behind Wax, told of his close encounter of the paranormal kind.

"I was setting up the bar on a Tuesday night when someone started banging on the door. Between tourists and friends, there is always someone trying to get in early for a drink. I was pretty busy so I just yelled for them to go away and come back later. The knocking continued, so I went over to the door and pulled it open, at the same time giving a look to let the person knocking know that I was unhappy. As the door comes open, I see a lady in a long dress crying. I ask her if she is all right, but she doesn't respond. I don't know what is wrong with her, so I bring her into the bar to grab a napkin for her eyes. I didn't turn around for more than a couple of seconds, but when I turned back with the napkin, she was gone.

"It was a little bizarre, but I don't think too much about it and lock the door back up, and then I go to the bar and start wiping down the glasses. I did the first one, set it down on the bar, finished the second one, and when I set it down, the first glass is gone. I looked all around, and it was nowhere in sight, so I just finished up the glasses that were still there.

"About fifteen minutes later, Vinnie K. walks in from the patio asking, 'What are you doing leaving glasses out?' He had found the glass I just wiped down sitting in the center of the pool table with a fresh lipstick stain on the rim. I've never been one to believe in ghosts, but I'm pretty sure I had a visit from the Water Witch of Appelrouth Lane."

The ghost known as The Water Witch haunts 2 Cents restaurant, pictured above. 420 Appelrouth Lane, below, is another location her spirit has been reported.

LOCAL LEGEND

David L. Sloan

Legends say the dining room of 2 Cents restaurant at 416 Appelrouth Lane was built over a small cemetery. Gravestones were used to elevate the main support beams. Old timers still claim at least one person was hanged from a nearby tree.

A STIFF DRINK ON CAROLINE STREET

David L. Sloan

Mr. Cheapee's Liquor Store now watches over the spirits at 423 Caroline Street. Former bars that existed here, all known for paranormal activity, include The Brick House, Jerky's, and Red's.

Kris Koshiol entered the bar and walked hurriedly toward the restroom. "Almost there," he told himself before rounding the foosball table and tugging the bathroom door handle. The door refused to budge. Knocking rapidly against the hollow wooden shell with his fist, Kris conveyed his urgency. "Open the door, I've got to go out here!" It seemed like an eternity before the door finally opened.

Safely seated, Kris' eyes wandered aimlessly around the men's room. To a newcomer, it might not have seemed different from any other downtown bathroom; but the locals were able to look past the damp floors and stained walls to see the things that made the bathroom at Jerky's bar so unique.

The urinal in Jerky's bathroom was probably the strangest in The Florida Keys. The urinal stood more than four feet tall, with a marble base and single drain, and it was able to accommodate two people at once while still affording privacy. Some old timers say this is the actual toilet Ernest Hemingway took from Sloppy Joes, but people in Key West say a lot of things while making room for their next drink.

Kris remained seated, but was soon overcome by the feeling of another presence and realized that he was not alone. A man in dark shoes stood inches before him, the tips of his shoes nearly stepping on Kris's feet. The warm bathroom turned ice cold. Kris's head jutted rapidly in an upward direction to find a suited man staring down at him with a confused look on his face.

"Get the hell out of here!" Kris yelled.

Kris was a strong guy, capable of taking on most of the bar if he wanted, but the stranger didn't budge.

"I said get the hell out of here!" he repeated, this time leaning forward in an attempt to shove the man back toward the urinal.

The man continued to give him a confused stare.

Moments later Kris emerged from the restroom and walked slowly to the bar. His face was pale and sickly as he relayed the story to Dennis, explaining that when he tried to shove the man his hands went right through him. "I almost fell off the toilet! And then the guy just turned toward the urinal and disappeared right through it!"

PHOTO: ROB O'NEAL

The unique 'double' urinal at 423 Caroline Street is rumored to be the actual piece of plumbing Ernest Hemingway removed from Sloppy Joe's Bar.

Over the course of the next several months both of the bar's owners had their share of bizarre encounters. Pauley was preparing to open one evening while talking with a friend who kept glancing toward the jukebox. She began to get fidgety, and her glances came with greater frequency until Pauley finally asked what was going on.

"Why is that man looking at us?" she asked.

"What are you talking about?"

"That man by the door. Do you know him?"

"I don't know what you're talking about, honey, but you don't need this." Pauley pulled Suzanne's drink away but could immediately tell she wasn't fooling around. Though the spirit was not visible to Pauley, he was starting to think that maybe the mystery man Kris had encountered had returned to the bar and decided to stick around for a while.

Larry Stanford was visiting from Naples a few weeks later and came to Jerky's with his brother for some beer and billiards. One game of pool turned into five, and it wasn't long before Larry headed in the direction of the men's room. As he worked his way toward the bathroom door, a guy walked in front of him. "I hope he doesn't lock the door. I really have to go," Larry thought.

The slender man in the yellow shirt entered the bathroom with Larry following close behind him. Larry entered with his only thought being which side of the urinal would be delegated to him. To his surprise, the entire room was vacant; the man had disappeared.

Other ghostly guests began to appear, including an older lady who stood quietly by the front door observing Dennis as he closed down at night. She visited with such frequency that the bar patrons were convinced she had a crush on Dennis. She always came in quietly, after the bar was closed and after the doors were locked.

Why so much activity at this particular location? Next time you find yourself walking down Caroline Street, stop into the old brick building for a bottle of liquor and tap your foot against the floor toward the back of the store. If you get the right spot, you will find it is hollow underneath.

According to local legend, the building was an icehouse. The hollow spot is over the pit where they once kept the ice. When the building doubled as a morgue, bodies awaiting burial were kept cool in the pit. It appears at least a few of the former occupants are sticking around until last call.

Monroe County Public Library

LOCAL LEGEND

Monroe County Public Library

The 400 block of Caroline Street is home to eight liquor establishments where ghosts have been reported. They include Kelly's, Grunts, Mr. Cheapee's, The Bull, The Whistle, The Garden of Eden, The Porch and The Other Side. Locals believe the water from a former tidal pond on the site continues to anchor the spirits to the area.

HAUNTED HEMINGWAY

ERNEST HEMINGWAY ... dead at 61.

Shotgun Blast Ends Hemingway's Life

The tragic death of beloved author Ernest Hemingway shocked the world, but some people are convinced Papa's spirit never left The Florida Keys and continues to haunt his favorite haunts from beyond the grave.

HAUNTED HEMINGWAY: THE WATCHER

David L. Sloan

Has Ernest Hemingway's spirit returned to the residence where he fell in love with Key West?

Monroe County Public Library

Built in 1919, the Casa Antigua is now home to the Pelican Poop Shoppe, but the building has seen quite a bit of activity over the years. It survived fires and hurricanes and has served as everything from a flophouse to a car dealership. It also has the distinction of having provided Pauline and Ernest Hemingway their first residence on the island.

It was April of 1928 when the writer and his wife arrived in Key West on a steamer ship. Ernest was to pick up his new Model A from the Trev-Mor Ford dealership that occupied this site. But when the shipment was delayed, the two were given lodging at The Trev-Mor Hotel on the second floor, above the garage. They stayed here for seven weeks, and during that time, Hemingway completed his first draft of "A Farewell to Arms." They fell in love with the island he called "St. Tropez of the poor," and remained in Key West for thirteen years.

Reports of hauntings at the Casa Antigua are common, and the location has become a regular stop for several ghost tours in town. This chapter takes the strange occurrences people have reported and tells the story from the perspective of the ghost.

The Casa Antigua at 314 Simonton Street was known as The Trev-Mor Hotel when Ernest Hemingway arrived in Key West. This became his first residence and the place he completed the first draft of A Farewell to Arms.

I watched with curiosity for several years as the tuxedo-clad gentleman led people past my residence, pausing briefly to point out the plaque reading, "On this site in 1886 nothing happened." His outfit was accented by a top hat and cape, and although we never spoke, I began to look forward to our nightly encounters.

Key West has always been dear to my soul. Her natural beauty, tropical climate, and ample supply of unusual people strolling down the lanes create rare magic. It was the people who first drew me from my room to the streets, and some years ago I began the nightly ritual of watching the world unfold from the comfort of my front door. I do my best work in the morning, as Key West afternoons prove a bit too humid for my taste. But later in the day, as the sun dips below the horizon and sea air cools the island, Key West has a beauty that could never be appreciated from the confines of a studio. Over the years, I have become accustomed to spending the better part of each evening passing time from my threshold at 314 Simonton Street.

One evening, the tour stopped before my home for a bit longer than usual. The group listened attentively and acted oblivious to my presence —

with the exception of one lady. She looked as if my being there startled her, though the others could sense that I was content to be left alone and listen in. People in Key West are pretty good at respecting the privacy of others. The guide pointed to the plaque, but I was distracted by the look this woman was giving me. I silently excused myself and headed back inside, leaving my friend in the top hat to tell his story.

The following night my interest was piqued as I observed my friend speaking of ghosts in the house. In all of my time here I have never seen a hint of such activity, but then again I am a bit of a skeptic. For nearly five years, the top-hatted tour guide and I had encountered each other on a nightly basis without speaking, but now I felt enough comfort to play along. It was a Friday evening and though I don't know what sparked my playfulness, I ducked behind the door as I saw the lantern turning from Eaton Street onto Simonton. Standing in my doorway the guide spoke of the plaque, went into the history of my residence, and then, "BOOM!"

I struck the closed door with all of my might, and judging by the screams on the other side it was quite a hit. My friend with the top hat was so startled that he had trouble telling his story, but I like to think we all had a good laugh about the episode. I will still bang against the door on occasion, just to keep them on their toes, of course, but for the most part I'm happy watching. Perhaps tonight I will listen to the whole story and see what this ghost business is all about.

Though Hemingway does not live in this house anymore, there are those who believe his spirit still does. A few months ago we had a psychic on the tour, and she approached me at the end to ask about the building with the large wooden doors. At the time, I was not sure which building she was talking about, but the psychic explained she had seen a ghost standing in the doorway. 'He was a broad shouldered man looking blankly toward the street,' she explained.

"Several weeks later a college student from Iowa asked about the man in the doorway, and two days later a teacher from England had the same question.

"Can you show me the door?' I asked. She walked me back to Simonton Street and pointed to the entrance of the Casa Antigua. Since we added this house to our tour, a number of people have seen the man; on occasion a loud knocking has been

35

heard, coming from inside the door. Some say it is the ghost of Ernest Hemingway, but if George Washington had slept here, they would probably say it was his spirit. During a time when the building served as an auto shop, some men died when batteries exploded in the heat. The ghost could be Hemingway, an unfortunate mechanic, or one of the many people who had the good fortune of staying in this home. We don't like to speculate, so let's just call him 'the watcher' as that is what he likes to do.

That seems a bit peculiar. They're talking about me as if I am a ghost...

State Of Florida Archives

LOCAL LEGEND

THE PIRATE'S WELL
KEY-WEST.

Dead men tell no tales? The Pirate's Well at 410 Caroline Street is believed to be the location of buried treasure. According to the Porter Family, a complete skeleton was found on the property during early excavations, complete with coins placed over the eyes. It was not unusual for two pirates to bury a treasure, but for only one to return knowing the location.

HAUNTED HEMINGWAY: ERNEST'S GHOST

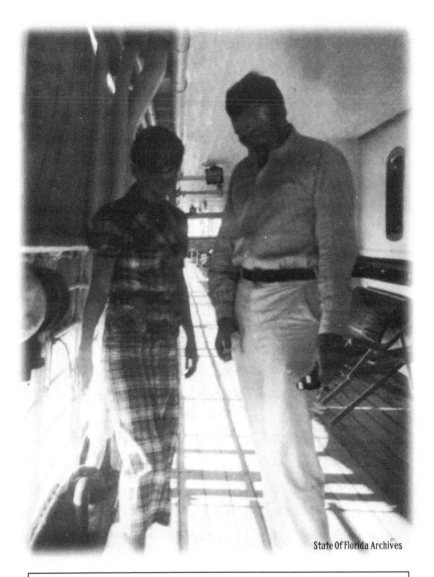

State Of Florida Archives

The ghosts of Ernest Hemingway and his second wife Pauline are sometimes seen by visitors to the Ernest Hemingway Home & Gardens at 907 Whitehead Street in Key West.

Six men gathered around the sturdy oak table that occupied the majority of the floor space on the drinking side of the Chart Room bar. The men tossed back mojitos and cracked the salty peanuts before disposing of their shells on the floor; each man had a devilish gleam in his eyes as he crafted a story that would one-up the tale told before it.

"Another mojito!" Frank beckoned to the bartender while puffing his chest and deepening his voice for effect.

"Make that two!" mimicked Lenny, his voice even deeper than Frank's.

Not to be outdone, the remaining four men followed suit with the drink orders, each one puffing their chest and lowering their voice with greater exaggeration than the one before them. When the sixth man had ordered, they simultaneously broke into a roar of laughter.

Valerie crushed mint, added sugar and rum, and began working her way around the table placing a drink before each of the bearded gentlemen. "There you go, Ernest, and here's one for you, Ernest, a mojito for Ernest, the same for Ernest, another for you Ernest, and last but not least, your mojito, Mr. Hemingway." They raised each glass to the center of the table and toasted the real Ernest Hemingway. These look-alikes were just brushing up for the story-telling competition the following day.

The drinks continued to flow as each took their turn spinning yarns about fish they had caught, girls they had landed, or drinks they had drunk. When Frank's turn came around, a solemn look went across his face and after many moments of uncomfortable silence he spoke. "Turn down the lights, Valerie." She couldn't tell if it was a demand or a request, but heeded his instructions and allowed the room to be cast in little more than shadows. Frank grasped the Ouija Board from a pile of games beneath the television and placed its components on the table.

"You are all aware that the Ouija Board has the power to connect us directly with the dead, but you may not know that the dead are already among us. The ashes of a man who used to frequent the Chart Room are interred in the very bar on which the mojitos you are enjoying were prepared. Next to his ashes are the remains of General Chapman of the Conch Republic, and this is also the very bar where the late, great Mel Fisher plotted his discovery of the Atocha." The men looked at Valerie for verification of the facts as she nodded her head and pointed to the burial spot on the bar.

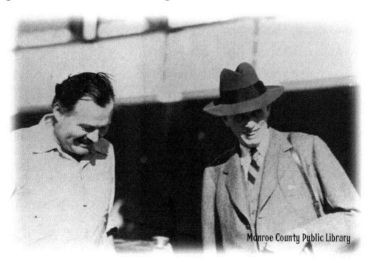

Monroe County Public Library

been known for her hauntings," he continued. "But earlier this very evening I came face to face with The Papa of all ghosts." The men leaned in closer, watching Frank's eyes for any signs he was lying. None could be detected.

"It was twenty-two minutes past eight o'clock when I approached the lighthouse. Crossing diagonally on Whitehead Street, I was amazed at the lack of activity around Hemingway's house, but relished the silence and welcomed it as an opportunity to reflect on the man we all love to imitate. As I walked toward the front gate, I imagined I was him coming home from an evening on the town. I could almost sense what he felt as my boat shoes shuffled along the sidewalk, and the scent of jasmine traveled gently through the air."

"I clasped my hands around the bars of the entry and stood for a few minutes gazing at the house. Just then I was distracted by a noise and noticed I was not alone. I cast my gaze to the shadow that drifted across the upper veranda, silently cursing the caretaker who had interrupted my solitude. As this person walked into the light, my thoughts went from anger to confusion as Old

43

Man Hemingway appeared on that veranda, not twenty yards in front me."

"Now before you accuse me of losing my marbles, there are a few things that should be explained. First off, I was not drinking. Secondly, there are people who work at that house who have talked about his ghost, experiencing everything from cold chills to the sound of a typewriter clacking away in the early morning. Thirdly, I've happened to notice that there are more than a few look-alikes wandering the streets of Key West this time of year, and I'm anything but gullible."

"I figured it was one of us getting a special after-hours tour of the place, so I called up to the balcony in hopes of joining in. 'Hey, Ernest!' I yelled, and the man walked to the edge of the balcony where his gaze met mine. I waved my arm back and forth and called out 'It's me, Frank.' He responded with a hearty wave and then right before my eyes became transparent and disappeared.

"I stood dumbfounded. Eventually I regained my composure and turned to walk away; but as my hands released their grip from the gate, an icy cold breeze blew against my back and rushed through the gate, stirring up leaves on the walk as it headed to the front door of his house.

"The hair on the back of my neck stood up for a good portion of my walk down Duval Street. It only happened on my way to meet you here tonight. You may call me crazy, but do I believe I met the ghost of Ernest Hemingway?" There was another moment of silence before the men followed Frank's gaze to the center of the table.

The glass cylinder of the Ouija Board's indicator rested firmly on "Yes."

Does the spirit of Ernest Hemingway appear in this 1965 photo taken by the Key West Property Appraiser's Office? (below)

LOCAL LEGEND

David L. Sloan

Local bars serve as the final resting place for at least a dozen former Key West residents. One island tradition includes mixing the ashes of the deceased into their favorite cocktails and placing them on a shelf over the bar so they can continue to drink with friends. Though ashes are the most common form for bar burials, a real human skeleton hangs behind the bar at Captain Tony's

HAUNTED HEMINGWAY: THE GHOST CAT

"How did she get in here? I thought you closed the doors before coming to bed." Nick wasn't angry, just a little surprised at the cat's presence. "I did close the doors," Joan said. "Maybe she was hiding under the bed."

Nick and Joan lived at 907 Whitehead Street. The 1851 house is best known as the home of Ernest Hemingway, but over the years the house has played host to a number of feline celebrities.

Kittens sun by the pool at the Ernest Hemingway Home & Gardens on Whitehead

Most cats have five toes on each front foot and four toes on each back foot. Genetics and inbreeding can cause additional digits, making the cats "polydactyl" in the scientific world, or simply "Hemingway cats" in Key West. Ernest was given his first six-toed cat by a sea captain, and many of the more than sixty cats living on the property today are descendants of the original.

Hemingway owned the home from 1931 until his death in 1961, but spent less time there after he purchased a residence in Cuba following his divorce from Pauline in 1939. The home was sold to Bernice Dickson in 1961, and was opened as a museum in 1964. It was during the early 1960s that Nick and Joan Di Lorenzo had the pleasure of renting a room above the old carriage house at the former Hemingway estate.

It seemed innocent enough when it first happened. Nick and Joan were lying in bed when a black and white tuxedo cat decided to join them. She hopped on the mattress between their feet and proceeded to walk across Nick's legs until she was comfortably perched at chest level. Paws kneading and motor purring, the cat was in heaven. Nick attempted to pet her, but she vanished into thin air. He wondered if he had been dreaming.

But it happened several more times, the last being early one morning. Nick felt the familiar paws across his chest and opened his eyes to see the same black and white cat with her face just inches from his nose. "Yowrlll." The cat stared into his eyes while emitting the sound, faded in color until she was transparent and then disappeared without a trace. Joan rolled over and gave Nick a tap.

"Can you open the door? The cat sounds like she wants to go out."

At this point, Nick knew that least one of Hemingway's cats has more than nine lives.

LOCAL LEGEND

State Of Florida Archives

Neighbors of The Ernest Hemingway Home & Gardens believe Ernest Hemingway is not the only ghost roaming the property. A woman matching the appearance of his second wife, Pauline Pfeiffer, has been seen smoking cigarettes near the front gate. When approached, she disappears, leaving only a partially burned cigarette behind — the same variety Pauline smoked. Pauline died on October 1, 1951.

HAUNTED HEMINGWAY: FINCA VIGIA, CUBA

PHOTO: ROB O'NEAL

The living room at Ernest Hemingway's former residence outside of Havana, Cuba. Employees of Finca Vigía believe the Pulitzer Prize winning author still has some unfinished business.

La Finca Vigia may not be a familiar estate to many Americans, but the name brings fear to the hearts of Cubans who have been employed there over the past several years. La Finca Vigia is best known as the former Cuban home of author Ernest Hemingway, and these employees believe his ghost is alive and well and still residing at La Finca.

The estate is quite sizeable and spans several acres with a variety of trees and lush vegetation. Deeded to the Cuban government in 1960, the home looks exactly as it did when Hemingway was living there. The original furniture, hunting trophies, manuscripts, shoes, pants and boots all give the impression he has only stepped away for a few minutes. Tropical paths meander across the estate and wind down the hills to reveal a guest home, swimming pool, pet cemetery and Papa's prize boat, the Pilar. But the paths are not the only things meandering around the famous estate.

Idania Rodriguez had worked at Finca for several years. She started at the gate giving directions for tour buses but eventually moved to the guesthouse, making sure people didn't try to walk away with any of the Hemingway belongings. It was here that she had her first ghostly encounter.

"It was the middle of the afternoon, and I was standing in the main room of the guest house. It is up on the second floor, so the only way to get in is from the steps outside, and then you can only come in a little bit because I am standing there to stop you. There was nobody on the steps at the time, so I was just waiting for people to come when I heard footsteps in the room behind me. Nobody is allowed back there, so I ran back to tell them to leave, but the footsteps stopped. It happened two more times that month and the last time I saw the shadow of a man, but no one was there. I told my boss I didn't like it there, so the next week they moved me to the main house."

Idania's responsibility in the main house was stopping people from grabbing Ernest's stuff through the open windows of the house, but her job also included preventing photos from being taken of the home's interior, or collecting $10 for each photo. The main house staff also had the responsibility of locking everything up at night, a task that would soon lead to Idania's departure.

"Nadia was closing up the entry room when I locked the windows of the bathroom and the library. I was standing by the shoe rack when I could feel someone behind me. I turned around, but no one was there. I started to walk back to the main room when I felt a cold breath by my ear and a voice that whispered, 'What are you doing here?' It was a man's voice. He spoke English. But there was no man around. I told Nadia, and she said it was just the ghost, but he was not bad. I was not sure I agreed."

Idania took to closing the exteriors of the house after the whispering incident. It seemed that nowhere on the estate was safe for her; perhaps the ghost had taken a liking to her dark eyes and the curls in her hair.

"It was a full moon the night that I saw him and I was the last one still closing. I was walking down the path to the pool when I heard a stick break on the ground behind me. When I turned around, I saw a man coming down the path. He was tall and red-faced, walking slowly. He was dressed in Bermudas, a light, baggy shirt, and leather sandals. I started to walk away from him but he continued to follow. The faster I walked away, the faster he followed me. When I realized who was following me, I went straight to the gate and left my key hanging on a palm tree before running home."

The Cuban Ministry of Tourism believes that the sightings of Ernest's ghost will benefit Finca Vigia. Idania Rodriguez resigned, and will not be revisiting Hemingway's Cuban estate any time soon.

LOCAL LEGEND

Michael Marrero

The Key West Fire House Museum at 1026 Grinnell Street has welcomed several unexpected visitors. A young Bahamian girl's spirit plays in the engine room at night and hides among the artifacts as she follows visitors on tours. A ghost named 'Frank' has identified himself to ghost hunting groups and psychics. The museum's Director of Operations believes a mischievous ghost in the station may be former Fire Chief, Joseph 'Bum' Farto.

THE DEVIL'S MASKS

62

"Help! Stop it! Get them off me!"

Rob ran from his bedroom in a panic that had become routine over the past several days. David jumped from his makeshift bed in the hallway, making a desperate attempt to figure out what was going on. "Spiders – the spiders are everywhere – come look at the bed."

Things had been pretty normal at 808 Simonton Street for the last year and a half. Three semi-professional men in their early thirties were sharing a three-bedroom apartment in Old Town, and their apartment seemed to become the site for an after-party for every late-night event they attended. Each of the men had a girlfriend and showed up to work on time, but they enjoyed their beer and told some interesting stories, even by Key West standards.

The problems started on a Monday morning in early March after David picked up a pair of masks from the Salvation Army store. The store was divided into various sections: men's clothes here, women's clothes there, furniture on this side, kids' stuff on that side. The masks were hidden behind a lime green couch from the late '60s and came as a pair — one female and one male. They stood nearly three feet tall, were hand carved from mahogany wood, and had sharp horns, pointed teeth, and demonic eyes. The $40 price tag seemed high for the Salvation Army, but David had to have them. He picked them up by the support wires spanning the backs of their heads and walked to the register.

"Did you see what he's getting?" one cashier asked another who was placing shirts on a nearby rack. The question rolled from her mouth with a slow, ominous tone that might indicate she knew something more, but David brushed it off as superstition. "Uhh-huhh." She replied, eyes glancing to the side and head raised as she looked cautiously at his new purchase. Maybe they were just jealous.

David felt good about his find as he hung the masks over his bed in Key West. He had never seen such unusual carvings, and the price really wasn't that bad. But that night, things started getting strange.

David had been sleeping with his door open so he could see the clock hanging above the front door in the living room. It was 5:00 am when he awoke, not with a start, not feeling tired, but simply awake, with the sense he was being watched. Looking toward the clock he was taken aback by the sight of a woman dressed in a Victorian hoop skirt holding her young daughter's hand and peering into his room with a look of concern.

"This isn't happening," he thought, but the image was clear as day. David had not been drinking that night. The episode lasted several minutes, with the daughter pulling on her mother's dress while pointing toward his room and the mother whispering in her daughter's ear. They eventually vanished, but it would not be the last time the duo paid a visit.

The following morning it happened again at precisely 5:00 a.m. After two more visits, David relocated his comforter to the space directly in front of Rob's room in the hallway at the other end of the house. "Maybe that will make them go away," he hoped. The ghosts were not frightening or aggressive, but they made it a bit unnerving to sleep.

David, wrapped in his blanket, positioned himself on the floor and closed his eyes. A chill filled the hallway but he refused to open his eyes, and then it happened. A dark shadow began to descend upon him, becoming more and more visible despite the fact his eyes were closed. It came within inches of his face before his eyes shot open, and the shadow disappeared. He closed his eyes again, and the creature returned.

David thought he was going crazy. "It's all in my head. None of this is real. It's just my imagination." He had almost convinced himself and was about to close his eyes again when Rob came running from his room screaming something about snakes. Things were not right at 808 Simonton Street.

This continued for several weeks. Rob was plagued by nightmares that included attacks by snakes, spiders, grasshoppers — even camels. David was visited by the dark shadow and the woman in the hoop skirt on a nightly basis. The masks were the obvious culprits for the activity, so the decision was made to get them out of the house. The nightmares and the apparitions stopped, and David returned to the Salvation Army hoping to find more information.

"Remember the wooden masks you used to have?" he asked the manager.

"They've been sold," was his cold reply.

"I know they've been sold, I'm the one who bought them," David explained. "I'm just trying to find out if you know anything about them. Do you know where they might have come from?"

The manager looked shocked. "They belonged to a girl who was in the other day. She was desperate to have them returned. She said she would do anything to get those masks back, and I mean *anything*. She stormed away pretty distraught when she found out they were gone, but she didn't leave any contact information."

So the possession of the masks remains a mystery. Were they crafted with evil intent? Or perhaps they were created for Voodoo rituals? Maybe they are a classic case of inanimate objects taking on the personalities of the dead? We may never know, but they will always serve as another subtle warning from the spirit world: be careful of the objects you possess, or one day they may end up possessing you.

The Devil's Masks spent more than a decade locked in a storage unit after this story was published. In 2013 they were moved to a local historical society and eventually placed on display with Ripley's Believe It or Not! at 108 Duval Street. Visitors who have viewed the masks at Ripley's Odditorium report animal-related nightmares and incidents of waking up to a dark shadow over their beds at the same time each night.

LOCAL LEGEND

Key West Light House, Key West, Fla.

Monroe County Public Library

Barbara Mabrity kept the lantern at the Key West Lighthouse shining for years and she apparently has no intention of retiring. Her ghost is said to climb all 88 steps of the lighthouse several times each night to make sure everything is shipshape. Visitors to the keeper's quarters in the lighthouse also encounter Key West's version of Typhoid Mary. Mary and her husband both fell victim to typhoid fever while employed on the site. Dozens of other ghosts have been seen roaming the lighthouse grounds, including two women seen walking hand in hand, an unknown soldier, and a pensive man near the lighthouse entrance.

THE SENTINEL: FORT ZACHARY TAYLOR

A haunted prison cell at Fort Zachary Taylor. Some visitors swear they hear a ghost whistling Dixie, despite the fact that Key West remained part of the Union during The Civil War.

"Give me some water," barked the raspy voice. His demand was a cross between anger and a plea for help, and was delivered with a tone that sent shivers down Abigail's spine. She jumped back, emitting a quiet yelp that drew the attention of her fellow tour mates. As the group moved toward a desolate brick room west of the fort's parade grounds, Abigail alone saw an image that would haunt her for months to come: an unkempt, sunburned man in uniform gripping his hands around the bars which turned the small room into a cell. Abigail looked back to the tour group and then the cell. He was gone.

Abigail was a regular visitor to Key West. Born in Memphis, she first came to the Keys in 1982 for a veterinary convention, fell in love with the place, and continued coming back two or three times a year. She was the first of her family to graduate college and the only to become a doctor, yet she still inherited the family business. Abigail came from a family of psychics. She could see ghosts, but was unable to control when or why they appeared.

Fort Zachary Taylor was built soon after Florida became a state, with construction starting in 1845. The three-story fort was not completed until 1866 – the 21-year delay was attributed to the remote location, shortages of men and supplies, the occasional hurricane, and yellow fever epidemics. The fort gained notoriety in 1861 when it was occupied by the Union Army, making Key West the southernmost city under Yankee control. Old Fort Taylor eventually outgrew her usefulness, and in time had levels removed, areas remodeled, and sections filled. The area is known today as one of the best beaches in Key West, but sections of the fort remain – sections that were restored with the help of a ghost. Abigail was unaware of the fort's haunted history until she spoke with the ranger who had guided her tour.

Monroe County Public Library

"What was the room that we passed by after entering the parade grounds?" she asked.

"The one you got spooked at?" Raymond replied.

Abigail smiled and asked him what he knew.

"People talk about ghosts around here, but I don't really believe in that stuff," he said. "I've heard strange noises after the park closes and seen a few things, but we're out here on an island, and it's probably just birds or shadows from the trees. The room you are wondering about was a holding cell. Not many prisoners passed through here, but they would have used the room to lock up soldiers who were drunk or disorderly."

Monroe County Public Library

Howard England and crew excavate .

Abigail plugged in her laptop that night for some research about the fort. In a Miami Herald article, she learned that the fort had been going to waste until Howard England, an engineer at the Naval Air Station, became curious about it in the 1970s. He began excavating in his free time and came across the largest collection of Civil War cannons in the nation. The antiquated weapons had been buried shortly before the Spanish-American War to strengthen the walls of the fort. The more Howard found, the more he wanted to know.

Howard told the Miami Herald:

"I used to try to figure out where things were in the excavation. Like, for example, how was the desalinization plant laid out? I couldn't tell. Where would certain things be?"

"I would dream about it at night. It would go through your mind again and again. You just can't keep it out of your mind."

This is where the helpful ghost came in.

"One day I was in room 13. We were still about halfway down in the digging. I heard a voice say, 'What be you looking for, Sonny?' I looked up, and there was this man standing next to me in a Civil War uniform, with a white beard."

"I said, 'Well, I'm looking for guns and things.' He said, 'Well, it's here. That's old Betsy. That was my gun. This was my room.'"

When Howard resumed digging, he found his first gun right where the spirit had told him. The spirit visited again, and Howard learned the location of the desalinization plant and eventually the soldier's name, which was Wendell Gardner.

Though Howard never researched the apparition who helped him excavate the fort, one day he was talking with a tourist who was fascinated by Key West and the Civil War.

"One of my ancestors served at this fort," the visitor said. "His name was Wendell Gardner."

Abigail completed her research and returned to the fort the following day, telling her boyfriend she wanted more sun. After a brief swim, she grabbed a bottle of water from the snack bar and headed back to the parade grounds where she met a ranger named Randy.

"What do you know about ghosts around here?" she asked him.

Randy was more than experienced with the fort's ghosts and shared stories from across the years with Abigail. He recounted tales of ghosts whistling Dixie, re-enactors who disappeared before your eyes, images in your peripheral vision, and soldiers who walked right through you.

"I get the strongest sensation back by the old tidal toilets," he said.

They talked for a while before walking by the cell from which Abigail had heard the voice. "You may have seen Lieutenant McClure," Randy explained. "He was charged with treason by the Union Army and locked up here. He vowed in his journal that he would avenge the imprisonment. The fact that he was asking for water could also indicate it was someone suffering from yellow fever, but I don't think there was a soldier here who would turn down a cold drink. "

Upon closer inspection of the room, Abigail found nothing. No desperate soldier, no sounds or sensations, just an empty cell. She thanked Randy for his input, but still questioned what was real and what she had imagined.

Abigail placed the remainder of her bottled water against the cell wall and began to walk away, convinced the entire episode had been imagined. Looking up toward the setting sun she walked in the direction of her bike but was interrupted by a somewhat familiar raspy voice. "Thanks, lady."

LOCAL LEGEND

Michael Marrero

The old jail played host to many names from Key West's paranormal past. Manuel Cabeza was pulled from his cell here and lynched by the KKK, inspiring a Voodoo curse on the island. Count Carl Von Cosel was held here after being discovered with the long dead body of Elena Hoyos. The surrounding grounds are charged with the residual hauntings of those who were sentenced here and the angry mobs that sometimes gathered in the early days. Though several hanging trees exist across the island, this was the site of the official Key West gallows. At least three of the gallows victims are still said to be hanging around.

THE LADY IN BLUE: CAPTAIN TONY'S SALOON

David L. Sloan

The tree growing through the roof of Captain Tony's Saloon at 428 Greene Street is said to be the place where pirates and adulterers were hanged. Ghostly activity is reported throughout the saloon and several bodies are buried on site.

"The bar you see just across the road is Captain Tony's Saloon. It was built way back in 1851, and it is said that from 1852 until 1875 it served not only as a bar, but also as an ice house and the city morgue." Patrick was entranced and stood close to Ray as he told the story.

Patrick had recently turned six and was excited to visit Key West for the first time. Unfortunately, his idea of fun was a little different than his mother's and Aunt Lindsay's, and after the second day of shopping on Duval Street, he started looking for his own entertainment. As they passed the La Concha Hotel, Patrick noticed a picture of a ghost and his eyes lit up. "Let's go on the ghost hunt!" he exclaimed.

The three entered the hotel lobby where a man named Frank gave them all the information they needed about the ghost tour. Patrick wanted to tour that night, but the ladies vetoed his decision in favor of a sunset cruise. "Give it a couple of days and he will forget all about it," Kathy kept saying. Patrick didn't forget.

"Are we going on the ghost hunt tonight?" He asked the question several times a day, picking up brochures everywhere they went until finally the ladies gave in. They joined the tour the following night, and though skeptical at first, Kathy found herself wanting more as Ray continued telling tales at the final stop of the evening.

"And if you take a look just above the roof of Captain Tony's you will see what looks like a tree," Ray continued. "If you look carefully you will notice that the tree grows right up through the ceiling of the bar. They don't cut it down because that is the original city hanging tree."

Patrick's eyes widened. He had seen that very tree earlier in the day.

"One unfortunate victim of the hanging tree still haunts the bar and is known as the lady in blue. Back in the day, Key West was a pretty tight-knit community, but it seems this lady had a few problems. One night she murdered her husband and her two children. It was a pretty brutal story, and some accounts even have her chopping them up into little pieces before retiring for the night. The town folk did not take too kindly to murder. As word spread about the crime, a lynch mob was formed to bring justice."

"It was just before dawn when they burst into the murderer's house and ripped her from the bed. The group marched her, clad only in her blue nightgown, down to the hanging tree where a noose was placed around her neck. Are all of you familiar with a noose?" The crowd nodded their heads as Ray continued his account.

"The knot of the noose serves two purposes. One is to create a loop so that the person doesn't slip away, but the other purpose is to crack the victim's neck so they die a little quicker. This lady's neck didn't break and she was strangled to death by the tension. It is said that as the life drained from her body, her face turned the same color blue as her nightgown. She haunts the bar to this very day."

"For reasons we don't really understand, she is most often seen in the ladies bathroom." Patrick's face turned white, and a small damp patch appeared on the front of his pants before trickling down his leg and forming a puddle on the Greene Street sidewalk below. The young boy's eyes grew wide and his entire body shook as if he were going into seizures. Ray stopped mid-sentence, simultaneously walking toward the boy and preparing to call 911 from his cell phone.

"It's okay, don't worry." Ray continued toward the boy as the voice spoke again, "It's okay, don't worry." It was Patrick's mom speaking as she picked up her son and walked to the rear of the tour group. Ray tried to follow and make sure everything was all right, but stopped short when a hand tugged his cape. "I'm his aunt. I'll explain everything when the ghost hunt is over."

Ray continued the story and answered questions when the tour was complete. Nobody was leaving without hearing what was wrong with the boy. With a little encouragement from the crowd, Lindsay stepped up beside Ray to explain.

"We've been trying to avoid the tour all week, but Patrick kept pestering us. Yesterday we were walking by Captain Tony's when Patrick spotted a skeleton behind the bar, so we went in for a soda and took a look around. My sister, Patrick's mom, decided to use the bathroom before we left, so I watched Patrick and then decided to go myself. Patrick decided he should go too, but we didn't want him going into the men's room alone. It's not like he still needs help going to the bathroom; we just didn't know who might be in there, and the ladies' room was empty so we sent him there while we watched the door."

"Patrick had had ghosts on the brain, so it didn't surprise us when he came out of the bathroom and said he was hearing voices. He kept talking about the lady in the bathroom who was trying to scare him. 'What did she say to you, honey?' his mom asked.

"She said to get out and that she doesn't like me."

"But no one is in the bathroom. Aunt Lindsay and I were just in there and it's empty."

"She said she wanted to cut me."

The crowd went silent when Lindsay shared this part of the story and even the skeptics had a shocked look on their faces. Most of the group headed into Captain Tony's for a drink, but not one of them dared to use the ladies room that night.

Captain Tony's as The Oldest Bar (above). The restrooms (below) are one of the scarier locations in the saloon today.

LOCAL LEGEND

PHOTO: ROB O'NEAL

Robert the Doll is the star attraction at the Fort East Martello Museum where letters arrive daily asking Robert's forgiveness for not paying him the respect he demands. Cameras malfunction, electronics misbehave, and Robert moves in his case. The museum also hosts the spirits of Civil War soldiers who fell victim to yellow fever and some visitors report entering a spirit portal or vortex that transports them to another dimension.

THE GHOST OF THE OVERSEAS HIGHWAY

PHOTO: ROB O'NEAL

She began to panic. Heavy rain hit the windshield, and the wipers could not keep up with the torrent of water. The blacktop road and pitch-dark sky blended seamlessly, and frequent bolts of lightning provided the only means of navigation. "Oh my god, I think I am going to die!"

Tammy Sigman came to Key West from Plano, Texas eight months after her husband passed away. It had been a difficult year with the children, and the southernmost city seemed like an ideal place to enjoy a week of sun and fun while leaving her troubles back home. The trip got off to a terrible start. The taxi that was to take her to the airport arrived late, she missed her first flight, and when she arrived at Miami International Airport, she discovered that her rental car was no longer available. "At least they didn't lose my bags," she thought to herself.

The rental car situation worked out when one became available in Fort Lauderdale, but it was almost midnight by the time Tammy hit the road. She was tired, cranky and like so many other tourists, she had no idea that it would take four more hours to reach Key West. "What else can go wrong?" she wondered. Then it started to rain.

U.S. Route 1 is breathtaking the first few times you see it. Like anything else, the novelty wears off when you drive it on a regular basis. After a few years of living in the Keys, you start to realize what a dangerous road it can be. Route 1 features a single lane in each direction, visitors driving slowly to enjoy the views, locals getting agitated and trying to pass, drunk drivers, deer in the roadway, poor lighting, and tropical weather. For Tammy, the sense of something disastrous started with the rain.

It was a light sprinkle at first, but the intensity soon picked up. She twisted the plastic knob in her rented Hyundai, adjusting the wiper speed from low to medium and eventually high, then turned down the radio before gripping both hands tightly around the wheel. Fiddling with the defroster only made things worse, and she began to feel a sense of panic.

"Just great!" she spoke aloud to no one in particular. "Here I am, a single mom stuck in a monsoon in the middle of nowhere, water on both sides of the road and a piece of junk rental car that won't even defrost right. Damn it!" She considered pulling to the side of the road, but that maneuver would require being able to see the side of the road. The blinding rain made it impossible to tell where the cement became sand or where the sand became water. Stopping seemed like a bad idea as well. "What if someone else can't see and plows into me from behind?" She turned off the radio and nearly broke the turn signal trying to get more speed out of the wipers. The storm's force increased and she found her nose just inches from the windshield in a futile effort to make out the lines of the road. "Somebody please help me," she begged, though no one else was in the car. At that moment taillights appeared on the road in front of her.

Tammy felt a hint of comfort knowing she was not the only one caught in this mess. Judging by the steady speed of the other vehicle, the driver was not having the same problems with defrosters, windshield wipers, and navigation. The red taillights emitted a soothing glow that cast down on the yellow dividing line. As she grew more comfortable with the situation, the lead car gradually increased its speed and Tammy soon found that she was driving out of the storm.

The mini convoy went on for twenty minutes before the rain was reduced to a sprinkle. Tammy wondered about the best way to thank her new friend; she considered stopping them for drinks or just passing by with a friendly honk and a hearty wave. A wave seemed like the most logical thing to do. "They might not even realize that they saved my life." She switched the wipers back to low and glanced down at the radio turning it on at a low volume. When she looked back to the road ahead of her the other car was gone.

State Of Florida Archives

"What the...? How did they disappear so quickly? Where did they go? Where *could* they go?"

Tammy increased her speed in hopes of catching up to say thanks, but the road ahead was empty. No turnoffs, no restaurants or shops, just a two-lane highway with water on both sides.

Tammy's vacation took a turn for the better, and she soon made Key West a regular get away, returning several times a year, but flying directly into Key West each time. One evening she met a couple at Mallory Square and the conversation turned to the terrible storm they encountered on the drive down. They described zero visibility, inability to see the road, fear of going into the ocean – and the appearance of a pair of red taillights on a mystery car that led them safely through the storm.

As the couple explained their brush with death a chill shot down Tammy's spine. "The car was there one second and gone the next," Greg explained. "It was the middle of the afternoon and there was nowhere it could have gone, so we pulled into a little bait shop and asked the old man if there were any other roads. He was a bit reserved at first, but when we told him about what had happened, he seemed to get a bit choked up and then just smiled at us. 'Looks like you got a little help from the ghost of the Overseas Highway.'"

Despite the unrivaled beauty of the Overseas Higway, the element of danger persists and several fatalaties occur each year. People say the mysterious car often described is driven by the ghost of someone who died driving off the Overseas Highway during a storm; they lost their entire family, and though they can never find peace, their ghost sticks around to make sure everyone who drives the Keys during a storm has a safe vacation.

Monroe County Public Library

LOCAL LEGEND

Michael Marrero

Dubbed 'the most haunted street in Key West,' Eaton Street is home to a restless sea captain who haunts the graveyard behind St. Paul's Church, playful children's spirits in the former church known as The Key West Theater, a doctor who continues his practice in spirit at The Old Town Manor, a nanny grieving the loss of children she cared for, and Robert the Doll's former residence – The Artist House. Sightings are common at all of the locations. Superstitious locals avoid certain areas of the street where a spirit portal is said to exist.

THE SEANCE

This is a personal account from the author of Haunted Key West.

Twelve people crowded into the Old Town guest room, preparing to join hands and attempt to contact the spirit world. While some were unable to conceal their nervousness, most of the participants had a gleam of excitement in their eyes. I looked at the situation with a mixture of hopefulness and skepticism. I was number thirteen.

Ghosts have been my passion ever since Mrs. Ubercedar thrilled our kindergarten class with tales of a Native American spirit who lived behind the walls of her 18th century Pennsylvania home. I was hooked after she showed us an actual photograph of the ghost. After two decades of reading everything paranormal I could get my hands on, I was fortunate enough to convert my passion into one of the best jobs in the world — telling ghost stories in Key West.

I was always a believer, but with this transition came an obligation to look at situations from a skeptic's point of view. At present, I believe that ghosts most definitely exist in our world, but in many cases the things we believe to be ghostly in nature can be explained by science or attributed to an overactive imagination. I guess you could say I am a believer who looks for other options.

I don't like Ouija Boards and I subscribe to the general belief that they can invite unwanted spirits. Over the years I have turned down many invitations to attempt contact with the other side using such a board. When an opportunity to join a séance in Key West's Artist House arose, it was just too good an opportunity to pass up.

The home was typical of those found in Old Town. It was a two-story, wooden structure built in the late 1800s and accented with wraparound balconies and pastel shutters. Two guests were waiting outside the etched glass door as I approached. The door slowly opened to reveal a man named Darryl.

"Good evening," he said with a staged Romanian accent straight out of a bad horror movie. There was a smile in his eyes as he led us up the staircase to the second floor. As the stairs creaked beneath our feet, Darryl introduced himself to Emily and Ernest. They were honeymooners from Virginia and had been invited by a palm reader they met just a few hours before.

Darryl and I needed no introduction as I had met him a number of times in the past while researching the ghosts that resided in his guesthouse.

He took us to the room where the others had gathered and my eyes glanced across the walls and ceiling looking for any signs of trickery. I recalled that this was one of the bedrooms, though the furniture had been removed for the séance. The room had only two signs that it had been lived in: a small, fringed table lamp and an Oriental carpet that sprawled the length of the floor.

Directly across the room was a staircase that spiraled up to a smaller bedroom in the turret above. Measuring no more than eight feet in diameter, the quaint upper room was surrounded by windows on all sides and made up the only section of the house at the third-floor level. Some would call the room charming, but the charm faded rapidly as the night went on.

Introductions were made and brief conversations filled the room, helping to ease some of the tension. A tall man with flowing brown hair and milky blue eyes asked that everyone be seated on the floor, side by side, creating a circle. Beside him were the different items to assist in welcoming the spirits, and a small leather satchel with a black woven drawstring. Jay was a warlock and would be leading the séance.

The lights suddenly went out, and the room was filled with a collective anxiety, much like people experience when a plane hits turbulence without warning. We quickly realized that the room had gone dark only because Renee had turned off the switch of the table lamp. Excitement replaced fear as she lit a white candle that sent shadows dancing across the faces of everyone in the circle. Renee was a psychic in town and had joined the séance to act as a medium — she would be the voice if any of the spirits wished to speak.

Jay spoke first, explaining the purpose of the séance and offering a prayer of protection to keep any evil spirits away. One by one he placed items on the table, explaining the purpose of each as he went along.

"The white candle represents fire. Fire can be used as a great tool, but it must also be respected or it can easily destroy. Keep your eyes on the flame as the spirits may use it to indicate their presence."

Incense was burned to represent the wind, a small vial of water was placed in the circle and the small leather satchel was revealed to contain soil from the ground to signify earth. With all four elements in place we joined hands and the spirits were summoned.

The candle flickered; some people felt a slight chill and Ernest even claimed to have the vision of a woman playing piano. Though no one would be proud to admit they had failed in their attempts to contact the spirit world, I could not help but think that I had just spent the last half hour sitting on an uncomfortable floor with nothing to show for it but two sweaty hands.

The lights were turned back on and we began discussing what we had or had not experienced when I noticed something out of the corner of my eye. It was a quick movement that I first thought was a person peeking down the staircase, but when I turned to look it was gone. Nothing strange about this, but a few seconds later it happened again. Once more I turned my head and nothing was there.

I never suspected ghosts, but the object continued to invade my peripheral vision and was becoming quite annoying. After several minutes of attempting to determine the source, I asked Darryl if I could have a look upstairs. He readily agreed.

Beginning my ascent, I looked to the top of the staircase expecting to find a ceiling fan that had been casting the odd shadow. As I hit the third step my gaze continued upwards but I was stopped dead in my tracks as my face, chest and knee hit the equivalent of a brick wall. Nothing was visible, but I was physically prevented from moving forward. A dense heat enveloped my entire body, causing my heart to beat faster than I ever imagined it could. I stood motionless for a moment and then heeded the advice of a little voice in my head. "Turn around and go down. Turn around and go down. Turn around and go down."

Jay gave me a curious glance as I stepped silently back into the room. "Why didn't you go up?" he asked.

The last thing I'm going to tell someone after a séance is that I was unable to ascend the staircase due to some supernatural force field that no one can see, so I decided to give myself a little reality check. "Why don't you give it a try?" I replied.

Jay began his ascent but was stopped in the same manner as he attempted to reach the fourth step. He turned and smiled before saying, "Something doesn't want us up there. Why don't we try it together?"

I joined Jay's side on the stairs and we both attempted to reach the top. There was a strong tension at first, but we were able to move forward one step at a time. The tension felt like we were pushing our weight against a giant balloon; the tension broke when we reached the top step and our surroundings became very surreal.

There was a strange calm about the room when we first entered but it was rapidly replaced by chaos as the space was filled with thousands of small gray objects that flew about the room. "Bats," I thought, but this was something very different. They were dark in color and consistent in size, but their shapes were constantly changing as they shot across the room in every direction. It seemed strange that we were untouched by the creatures as they flew about so erratically; it seemed even more strange when we realized they were going right through us.

Jay and I stared blankly at each other. There was so much confusion that fear had no time to set in. I had the feeling that time was standing still as the gray streaks continued to swoop around us in silence, but then the silence was broken by a shrill scream.

"No! Stop It! Get Out! Leave!" It was Renee screaming from the room below. Jay and I rushed down the stairs as the bizarre wisps escaped through closed windows by the hundreds. When we reached Renee, she was shaking. "I don't know what that was, but I have never felt something so strong in all of my life. I've got to get out of here." Everyone left, uncertain about what had just happened.

Three years passed, and I learned to keep the story to myself as most people found it less than believable. One night the story resurfaced when I was talking to a medium who stuck around to chat after the tour.

"There are many spirits that wish to make contact from the other side," she explained. "When you hold a séance these spirits will gather above in hopes of being called upon. Look at the séance as a doctor's office and the area directly above it as a waiting room. Though the séance was over, many of the spirits were still in the waiting room hoping they would be called. When you penetrated the protective bubble, you entered the waiting room of the spirit world."

We had held the séance in hopes of contacting Robert the Doll but got much more than we bargained for.

LOCAL LEGEND

Gregory Hummel

Known as The Oldest House, one of the oldest surviving structures on the island was home to the Watlington family. Captain Watlington still haunts the captain's office, while his children's ghosts play with marbles on the stairs. A mysterious rocking chair at the home moves on its own. One local legend claims Elena Hoyos was buried on the property after her body was discovered in the possession of Count Von Cosel.

Von Cosel: The Secret Of Elena's Tomb

Elena Hoyos in a photograph taken outside her school. Young Elena never knew the place she would earn in history after meeting Dr. Karl Tanzler Von Cosel.

Monroe County Public Library Archive

Doctor? Scientist? Hopeless romantic? Mad man? More than half a century later, the people of Key West are still uncertain about the motives of Karl Tanzler Von Cosel.

Elena Hoyos was a beautiful young woman. Raised in a well-to-do Cuban family that had fallen on hard times in Key West, Elena had raven black ringlets of hair and was described as "full of life" by all who knew her. Charming and graceful, she seemed to have it all, including a handsome young husband named Luis Mesa. The newlyweds had a promising future together and were preparing for their first child when things took a turn for the worse.

Young Elena had a miscarriage, and shortly after, she became ill and was diagnosed with tuberculosis; at that time, tuberculosis was a contagious and incurable disease. Her husband left her, and due to her parents' misfortune, they were unable to provide Elena with the care she needed.

Enter Count Karl Von Cosel.

Count Von Cosel was a self-proclaimed Count, as well as many other things. A German citizen, his real name was Karl Tanzler. He was well read in many subjects, but it is doubtful that he had any real schooling in the various trades he practiced. One of those fields was medicine, and it was his work with x-rays that got him a job at the Marine Hospital and led to his first chance encounter with Elena.

In his memoirs, the Count often talked of his search for a bride. Though he already had a wife and two children in Zephyrhills, Florida, he left them to search for his soul mate. He would know her when he found her, for she had visited him before.

When Elena walked into the Marine Hospital, Count Von Cosel's thoughts flashed back to Germany thirty years prior. Ten years before Elena was born, her apparition appeared to Karl with the ghost of one of Von Cosel's ancestors, the Countess Anna. The Countess told him of his destiny, and as the veil was lifted on the mysterious apparition, he saw the face of Elena, his bride to be.

Realizing he had finally met his future bride, the Count was quite nervous about taking her blood sample and chest x-ray. But this excitement soon turned to sorrow. The prognosis was terrible. The tuberculosis had advanced and death was certain, but Von Cosel would not give up on his newfound love quite so easily.

He visited her every day, and provided radiation treatments free of charge. He showered her with gifts and expressed his desire to marry her, but Elena always declined, saying she was ill, and perhaps they would marry once she recovered. She never did.

Elena died just days before Halloween and was buried in a simple tomb. The Count could not bear to think of her precious body rotting in the ground. With her father's permission, he had the body exhumed and properly embalmed, then placed in a special coffin and crypt equipped complete with a telephone, so he could speak to his deceased love. He visited her crypt daily. He believed that he could communicate with her spirit, and he believed that he and Elena had devised a plan to reunite Elena's body and soul.

Immortal Kisses Were His Goal

Like the Hero of De Maupassant's Weird Story, Old Scientist Van Cosel Tried to Lure From the Dead His Young Beloved, Stole Her Body From the Tomb, Preserved It With Wax, Slept Beside It for 7 Years, Claims to Have Revived Her Twice and Still Hopes to Succeed Again

Seventy-Two-Old Karl Tanzler Van Cosel, Scientist, Who Resolved to Steal Life, Like the Hero of De Maupassant's Fictional Madman, Who Sought Eternal Kisses by Bringing a Dead Woman to Life.

The Body of Elena Hoyos, Nine Years Dead, Partly Preserved by Wax, Enshrined in the Retreat of The Old Scientist, Who Next, With His X-rays, Tried for Seven Years to Bring It Back to Life.

HALF a century ago, Guy de Maupassant wrote a famous short story, "The Phase of Love," the tale of a man who believed he had brought back to life a dead woman. The idea was so fantastic, unscientific and "impossible" that few were surprised when its author was taken soon after to a Parisian lunatic asylum, to die.

In Key West, Florida, the other day, officers of the law took away from an elderly German scientist, Karl Tanzler Von Cosel, the body of Elena Milagro Hoyos, an attractive young matron who had died nine years ago.

For the last seven years he had been "persuading and coaxing"...

Unable to Bear the Thought of a Grave as Elena's Last Resting Place, Van Cosel Built This Tomb From Which He Later Stole the Body.

The Wingless Airplane Used for Secretly Transporting the Dead Woman From Her Tomb to the Old Scientist's Home.

Newspapers around the world covered the bizarre Key West story of Elena Hoyos and Count Karl Von Cosel.

115

When the time came, Karl knew what he must do. By the light of the moon, he slipped into the graveyard and removed her body from its tomb. Transporting her in cart fashioned from an airplane fuselage, Von Cosel took the body home and began the process of restoring Elena's body. According to his memoirs, Elena's spirit now began to speak to him, providing instructions on the recreation of her body.

The funeral home had really botched the job of embalming. When Karl opened her inner coffin, he found Elena's body in an advanced state of decomposition. Most of her skin was torn off, having stuck to the now fallen lining of the coffin.

The process of rebuilding Elena's body was difficult, but the Count was able to reconstruct her face with mortician's wax and plaster. Her head was completed with two glass eyeballs and locks of her own hair. People who later saw her said that the face was an incredible likeness.

The body, however, presented a problem. When her corpse was removed from the coffin, it weighed a mere 40 lbs. Von Cosel had to bring the weight to at least 100 pounds, and did so by stuffing her body with rags and saturating her in a custom-made tank filled with embalming fluids and antiseptics. Elena's decaying skin was replaced with silk, as this was the only material as smooth to the touch as her own skin had been. This was very important to the Count, as we would later discover.

For the next seven years, Elena shared a bed with the Count in a small, out-of-the-way shack on Flagler Avenue. Rumors began to circulate around town about the strange happenings in the Count's house, and the stories eventually reached Elena's sister Nana. Nana went to investigate, and upon peering through the Count's window, she stood in disbelief.

Count Von Cosel sat in the small room playing a melody on the organ. In the bed next to him was a fully constructed Elena, wearing a wedding dress with a ring on her finger. Her sister had been dead for nine years.

Police arrested Von Cosel was charged him with wanton and willful destruction of a tomb. Elena's body was placed on display in the local funeral chapel, where over 6,800 people came to see the body. Key West became a media circus and the story spread around the world.

The case never went to trial. A heartbroken

Count Von Cosel returned to Zephyrhills, and lived just miles from his first wife. He spent his remaining days writing his memoirs. Hours after the Count had fled Key West, a mysterious explosion blew up the crypt he had crafted for Elena, which now stood vacant.

Monroe County Public Library Archive

Because of all of the media hype, as well as the Count's obsession, Elena's body was cut into small pieces and placed in an 18-inch long box. She was buried at midnight in a secret location. Some people say she is in the cemetery, while others say she is under the Oldest House - but no one will ever be sure. All three men involved in her burial

118

have since taken that secret to their graves.

Count Von Cosel eventually died as well. After his death, doctors who had examined Elena's body released some disturbing news. Count Von Cosel had consummated his marriage to Elena.

As an appropriate ending to the story of a love that would not die, when Karl's body was found, he was lying on top of an open coffin, holding in his arms a replica of Elena de Hoyos.

The search for Elena's ghost continues, and though stories arise from time to time claiming to know where her presence is, none have been verified. Nonetheless, the spirit of Elena will always live on in Key West.

Monroe County Public Library Archive

SEPTEMBER 25¢

fantastic
ADVENTURES

THE SECRET OF ELENA'S TOMB
by KARL TANZLER VON COSEL

Count Von Cosel published his version of events in great detail in a 1947 pulp called Fantastic Adventures. The same story is now published as The Lost Diary of Count Von Cosel.

120

Count Von Cosel's secret was discovered in an old slaughterhouse he had converted into a laboratory near Rest Beach. Elena Hoyos was found wearing a wedding dress.

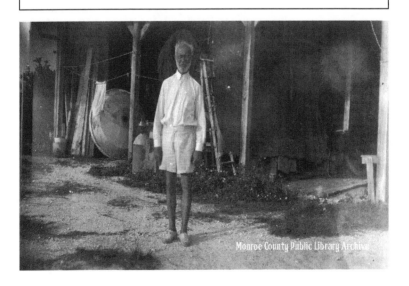

Above, Elena Hoyos as she looked while alive., Von Cosel (right) used the wingless airplane (below) to transport Elena's body around town without being detected.

Elena's Airship.

ABOUT THE AUTHOR

PHOTO: NICK DOLL

David L. Sloan launched his paranormal career in 1996, founding one of North America's first ghost tours in Key West, Florida. He has South Florida's largest collection of haunted objects, authored a dozen books, studied Santeria and Voodoo, and has dealt firsthand with dark entities and spirit possession.

Sloan remains the authority on the haunted history of Key West and The Florida Keys. He is frequently featured on national television and is a regular on several paranormal radio programs. David lives in Key West and operates The Key West Ghost Hunt: www.keywestghosthunt.com.

Message Sloan directly: david@phantompress.com.

If you enjoyed Haunted Key West, please leave a review on Amazon and share your thoughts on social media.

Additional copies available at local stores throughout the Florida Keys.

Outside of the Florida Keys, visit Amazon.com

Also available from David L. Sloan:

Ghosts Of Key West
Robert The Doll
The Lost Diary of Count Von Cosel
The Key West Bucket List
The Key West Key Lime Pie Cookbook
Quit Your Job & Move To Key West
Key West 101
The Key West Hangover Survival Guide
The Havana, Cuba Bucket List

GHOSTS
OF KEY WEST

David L. Sloan

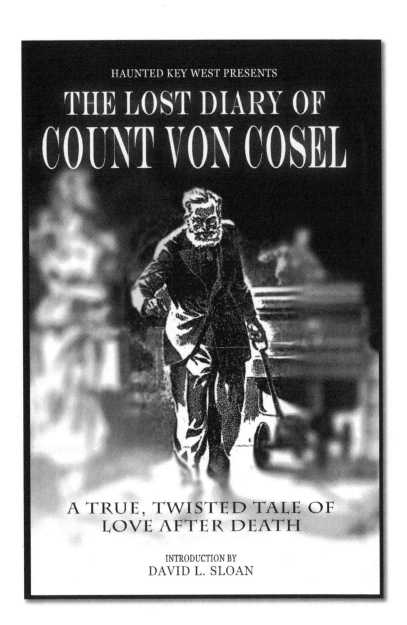

HAUNTED KEY WEST PRESENTS

THE LOST DIARY OF
COUNT VON COSEL

A TRUE, TWISTED TALE OF
LOVE AFTER DEATH

INTRODUCTION BY
DAVID L. SLOAN

ROBERT
THE
DOLL

HAPPY HAUNTINGS

THE END

93683021R00072

Made in the USA
Columbia, SC
18 April 2018